The
CRUCIFIXION
in
Irish
Art

THE
CRUCIFIXION
in Irish Art

Fifty selected examples
from the ninth to
the twentieth century

Peter Harbison

MOREHOUSE PUBLISHING

the columba press

Morehouse Publishing
P.O. Box 1321
Harrisburg, PA 17105

The Columba Press
55A Spruce Avenue
Stillorgan Industrial Park
Blackrock, Co. Dublin, Ireland

*Morehouse Publishing is a division
of The Morehouse Group.*

Columba ISBN 1-85607-278-9

Design by Corey Kent
Cover photo: Harry Clarke stained glass windows, St. Joseph's Church,
Terenure, Dublin, by Michael Blake

LIBRARY OF CONGRESS CATALOGING-IN-PUBLICATION DATA

Harbison, Peter.
    The crucifixion in Irish art : fifty selected examples from the ninth to
the twentieth century / Peter Harbison.
        p.   cm.
    ISBN 0-8192-1815-4 (alk. paper)
    1. Art, Irish. 2. Jesus Christ—Crucifixion—Art. I. Title.
N6782.H36 2000
704.9'4853'09415—dc21   99-35370
                                                          CIP

Acknowledgments

In addition to those thanked in the notes and photographic acknowledgments, I would like to express my most sincere thanks to the following who have been so helpful in one way or another in the preparation of this book over a ten-year period: the Augustinian Friary, Ballyhaunis; Cormac Bourke, Ulster Museum, Belfast; the Convent of Mercy, Cookstown; Derek Cullen and the photographic section, Bord Fáilte, Dublin; Barbara Dawson and Liz Forster, Hugh Lane Municipal Gallery, Dublin; Mrs. Kathleen Fitzgibbon, Mitchelstown; Prof. Patrick Fottrell, National University of Ireland, Galway; John Kennedy, The Green Studio; Heather King; Margaret McCullagh, Northern Ireland Tourist Board, Belfast; Ciarán McGonigal, Director of the Hunt Museum in Limerick; Marie McFeeley, National Gallery of Ireland, Dublin; Dr. Peter Ochsenbein, Abbey Library of St. Gall; Pádraig Ó hEailidhe, Dublin; Aoife O'Shea, National Museum of Ireland, Dublin; the parish priests of St. Joseph's, Terenure, Dublin, Kingscourt, Co. Cavan, and Navan, Co. Meath; the President and Council, and the librarian, Siobhán Ó Raiffertaigh, of the Royal Irish Academy, Dublin; Patrick Pye; Tony Roche and John Scarry of Dúchas, The Heritage Service; the late Brother Benedict Tutty, O.S.B., Glenstal; and Dr. Michael Wynne, Dublin.

Introduction

The crucifixion, being a central theme of Christian thought, is the only religious event or scene that has been represented in Irish art in virtually every century from the year 800 down to the present day. Crucifixes and crucifixion scenes thus provide an ideal and consistent yardstick against which we can measure the achievements of Irish artists and craftsmen during the last dozen centuries or so. They can reflect not only the changes in art styles throughout this period, but also—through individual characteristics and the accompanying figures and objects—the changing theology down the years.

Indeed, it could be said that the representations illustrated also provide us with a visual lesson in Irish history, in that a study of the ups and downs of their artistic quality mirrors the vacillating fortunes, as well as the comparative strengths and weaknesses, of Irish culture.

Despite many assertions to the contrary, there are no Irish crucifixion scenes that can be reliably shown to be earlier than 800. This is a period in Ireland's history when the country's religious schools brought forth a Johannes Scotus Eriugena who could astound the world with his learning, when craftsmen produced such gems as the Ardagh and Derrynaflan chalices, and when monks created the Book of Kells. Such masterpieces were not the products of an Ireland in isolation, but one in constant communication with other parts of Europe—for, as we know, the sea connects more than it divides. These relationships with the outside world, then and later, brought new images to Ireland that in turn gave fresh impulses to Irish artists. Indeed, throughout their history, Irish artists have always been seen to rise to their greatest heights when reacting positively, and adapting themselves, to new stimuli from abroad.

Such was the case when we come across the earliest examples of the crucifixion in Ireland during the ninth century. The Irish artist, who traditionally inclined toward the abstract and the stylized, was coming to grips in earnest then, for the first time, with the reproduction of the human figure in something resembling its natural shape, as seen on the High Crosses (e.g., No. 2). Nevertheless, the Celtic artist could not resist the temptation to stylize the human figure according to his own canons and to render it as an ornamental pattern (e.g., Nos. 1 and 3). For a time, the pagan Vikings, coursing the waves at night and the countryside by day, dealt a body blow to the practice of religious art, but the resilience of the country's craftsmen permitted them to participate vigorously in the great swell of Romanesque culture and decoration that took much of Europe by storm in the eleventh and twelfth centuries (e.g., Nos. 6 and 11). Religious art in Ireland was still able to transcend the shock of the early years of the Norman invasion in the last quarter of the twelfth century, but shortly afterward much of the individuality of the Irish craftsmen disappeared, and Ireland entered the stream of international Gothic. By the thirteenth century, Irish and Norman societies were both so heavily involved in the struggle for political and military survival that the resources necessary for commissioning works of art were not available to either side, which is why scarcely a single crucifixion can be reliably assigned to the thirteenth century.

By the early fourteenth century, things had settled down sufficiently for the Normans to be able to add scenes of crucifixion to their tombstones (e.g., No. 13). The Black Death of 1348–50 played havoc with Norman stability, but the later parts of the century saw a Gaelic revival in both poetry and the visual arts, particularly in the western half of the country. Throughout the fifteenth century, Ireland experienced an unparalleled building fever, which spilled over into the field of architectural and tomb decoration (e.g., Nos. 16 and 18). It manifested itself in high standards of sculpture in stone and metalwork, among both the Anglo-Irish of the East (e.g., No. 17) and the pure Irish of the West (e.g., No. 19)—again, not without outside stimulus. One of the last high points of Irish medieval sculpture, which already betrays

Renaissance influence (e.g., No. 24), coincides with the closure of the Irish monasteries by Henry VIII.

The effects of the Reformation and the Irish struggle against Elizabethan domination make themselves felt in the gradual decline of Irish art from participation in the international Gothic style (e.g., No. 19) to the level of folk art, sometimes of considerable vitality (e.g., No. 26), but also occasionally of paltry simplicity (e.g., No. 27). This trend intensified in the seventeenth century, when we find a number of simple yet charming crucifixion scenes decorating tombs and buildings (e.g., Nos. 29–31). Only on rare occasions, as on the Athcarne Cross (No. 32), was the Irish sculptor able to rise above the norm.

The first half of the eighteenth century saw—with a few exceptions (e.g., No. 35)—a Protestant minority more interested in the world of secular art and an Irish peasant majority reduced to the secret practice of its religion, causing a reduction in the size of crucifixes to pieces that could be hidden on the person, as evidenced by the so-called Penal Crosses (e.g., No. 38). But the second half of the century saw a relaxation of religious persecution, and the Catholic majority could show their adherence to their faith at least in death, as witnessed by the number of crucifixion scenes on tombstones (e.g., No. 36). As with Athcarne (No. 32) in the previous century, Edward Smyth's crucifix in Navan (No. 37) shows the Irish sculptor able to rise above the folk norm that surrounded him.

The Catholic Emancipation in 1829 allowed for a great increase in church building which, for lack of more traditional models, turned to Italy for its often sentimental furnishings. The rediscovery of the Celtic past throughout the second half of the century saw an upsurge in tombstones imitating the form of the old Celtic cross, often decorated with crucifixions, some of which are of considerable interest (e.g., No. 41).

Our own century has experienced a strong tendency away from religious representations in art. Those few artists who, through inner conviction, have managed to react to these tendencies have had to rely largely on commissions for church furnishings in order to have an opportunity to express themselves. But this they have done successfully, producing works of art in a modern style that can stand comparison with much of what has been produced in many other parts of Europe. Indeed, some exciting products of the modern Irish school of stained-glass artists (e.g., Nos. 44 and 46-47) find few equals anywhere.

When we take tombstones and church furnishings into account, many thousands of crucifixes and crucifixions can be said to have survived in Ireland from the ninth century onward. A small book of this size can, naturally, reproduce only a small percentage of these. Quality and visual interest were not the only criteria for inclusion here. An effort has been made to provide a wide historical and geographical range with a concentration, where possible, on reasonably well-dated monuments. At the same time, an attempt was made to produce examples typical of the period that bear witness to the religious fervor of those who commissioned the art. In addition, attention has been paid to the wide variety of media that offer themselves (manuscripts, metal-work, wood, stone, and glass) and to the extensive choice of monuments on which the crucifixion appears (crosses, tombstones, churches, and buildings). Although criticism may be leveled at the actual choices, for which the author alone is responsible, it is hoped nevertheless that the selections will stimulate not only an appreciation of the ebb and flow of Irish art, but also some inner reflection on the subject matter illustrated. The hope could be expressed that the samples chosen here might act as an inspiration for Irish artists to look at some of the better examples of earlier centuries—as Evie Hone (No. 46) and Imogen Stuart (No. 50) have done—and to produce crucifixion scenes that, in turn, might ennoble the quality of future generations. Many of the sentimental figures on today's tombstones, and other monuments and illustrations of a religious nature, are unlikely to do so!

NOTE: In the descriptions that follow, right and left refer to what the observer sees as right and left in the illustrations, except when referring to the sides or parts of the body of a person, e.g., Christ's left side or his right arm.

The
CRUCIFIXION
in
Irish
Art

1. Abbey Library of St. Gall

I. St. Gall, Switzerland

Circa 800
Abbey Library, Codex 51, p. 266

What is perhaps the earliest surviving Irish representation of the crucifixion is preserved not in Ireland but in the Abbey Library of St. Gall
in Switzerland. It decorates a manuscript taken there, doubtless by an
Irish monk, in the ninth century. Like the roughly contemporary Book
of Kells, it is richly colored and displays the characteristically Celtic
genius for ornamentation and stylization. Christ's body is swaddled in
a deceptively unanalyzable weave of ribbons designed by an artist who is
as much bent on avoiding symmetry as he is on intentionally distorting
the human figure. This he does by displacing downward, and seemingly
detaching, Christ's small and flexed legs as they emerge (unexpectedly
from the right) at the bottom of the folds. Christ's hair, too, is purely
ornamental, and his nose is shown in Picassoesque profile on his
beardless face. He is flanked by four figures who will continue to
accompany him for centuries, two book-holding angels above the arms
and two very different figures below. On the bottom left, as we look at
it, Stephaton offers Christ vinegar in a half-moon-shaped vessel on the
end of a tall pole; on the bottom right, Longinus casts his lance into
Christ's left side—rather than the right, which we have come to expect.
This feature, found on many early Irish crucifixion scenes, may stem
from the account in the apocryphal Passion of Longinus telling how he
split Christ's heart in twain, which he could have done only if he had
pierced Christ's left side. A small zigzag line, close to the head of the
spear that Longinus holds, alludes to the old legend that his diseased
eyes were instantly cured when the blood and water issuing from
Christ's wound fell upon them. The stark right angles of Christ's body
and cross, already softened by the undulating swirls of his garment, are
counterbalanced by the triangular composition of the pole and lance,
continued upward by the twin ribbons above Christ's shoulder.

2. Monasterboice, County Louth
Second half of the ninth century
Muiredach's Cross, West Face

Many of the great stone High Crosses of Ireland portray the figure of the crucified Christ in a much more realistic form than does the St. Gall manuscript (No. 1), suggesting that the high-relief carving of the crucifixion on Muiredach's Cross at Monasterboice, shown here, is much closer to a sculpted Carolingian model on the continent than is the St. Gall depiction. Indeed, the strength of the foreign influences at work here can best be judged by the fact that the High Crosses show Irish craftsmen overcoming for the first time their traditional dislike of representing the human form in the naturalistic style of the Greeks and Romans. Such style was, itself, the very antithesis of the Celtic love of stylization and geometrical decoration. The sculptor of Muiredach's Cross rejects the loincloth often found at this period and shows Christ, instead, clad in what looks like a pair of short trousers, with his legs bound by a rope. The High Cross shares with the manuscript page the lance and sponge-bearers as well as the accompanying angels, but it adds further figures that tell us much about the theological interpretation of the crucifixion in ninth-century Ireland. Underneath Christ's left hand is a kneeling figure with its back to Christ, clutching what seems to be a small child. The figure may be interpreted as Gaia, the personification of earth. Beneath Christ's right hand is a small seated figure that may, correspondingly, be taken as Tellus, or Ocean, the personification of water. When we combine these two figures with the (now much-worn) faces of the Sun and Moon beside Christ's knees, we realize that we have here four elements of the universe. The crucifixion was, therefore, being interpreted by the Irish monks as the central event in the history of the cosmos, represented in symbolical form by the ring or circle of the cross.

2. P. Harbison

3. National Museum of Ireland, Dublin

3. St. John's Abbey, near Athlone, County Roscommon
Ninth century bronze plaque in the National Museum, Dublin

No class of early Irish metalwork shows a more contrasting symbiosis, nor a happier union, of the human figure and ornamental patterns than the bronze crucifixion plaques. Of these, the one found at St. John's Abbey, near Athlone, is by far the earliest (compare also Nos. 6 and 7). Our gaze is immediately drawn to the outsize head of Christ in high relief, because the smooth and softly modeled surfaces of his somberly passionate face offer us calm and repose in the midst of the maelstrom that surrounds it on all sides. The Celtic artist shows his reversion away from the naturalistic sculpture of the High Crosses (e.g., No. 2) toward more ornamental patterns by decorating Christ's breast with lively spirals in relief, which provide the mechanism for attaching the arms to the body. By comparison, our eyes find rest once more in the flat surface of the lower part of Christ's robe, into which a profusion of interlace, fretwork, and spiral motifs has been carved. Indeed, Christ's body and garment, together with the wings of the ministering angels above, are a veritable celebration of ornament, which once may have had a symbolic meaning that is now lost to us. Each of the angels holds in its hands an object that might be construed as an instrument of the Passion. Beneath Christ's right arm we find Stephaton holding up a pole that passes, unseen, behind the spiral decoration on Christ's breast, before emerging again to hold the vinegar in a half-rounded vessel visible beneath Christ's chin. On the other side, Longinus thrusts his lance almost vertically upward into Christ's armpit. The heads of these two flanking figures sit awkwardly sideways, perhaps modeled on a manuscript prototype akin to that of the St. Gall gospels (No. 1).

4. Carndonagh, County Donegal
Ninth (?) century
High Cross

On most Irish High Crosses, the Crucifixion naturally occupies the central position at the crossing of the arms and shaft. Among the few exceptions is the cross outside the Church of Ireland grounds at Carndonagh, where it is the shaft of the east face that bears a crucifixion scene above three leftward-turning figures. Christ is clad in a robe to the knees, and his head appears to be ringed by a cowl or a hood—reminiscent of the outline on the St. John's Abbey bronze plaque (No. 3). His arms, which emerge curiously close to the center of the chest, separate the larger figures beneath from the two on a smaller scale above. Though wingless, the latter two—flanking Christ's head—are most likely angels, but the side figures beneath Christ's arms probably introduce us to two new characters. That on the right (under Christ's left hand) has a small bird pecking at the top of his head. The object above the head of the left-hand figure of the pair is larger, though less clear, causing Christ's right hand to be raised higher to make room for it. But comparison with an illustration of the crucifixion in a manuscript at Würzburg (Germany) suggests that the object could be an angel accompanying the good thief, so that the figure under Christ's left arm probably represents the bad thief. The three figures facing left at the bottom of the shaft may well be the holy women coming to the tomb, a symbolic way, known from the ninth century onward, of indicating the Resurrection. If this interpretation be correct, the figures could suggest a possible date with which to contradict the widely-held view that this is the earliest surviving High Cross, dating from as early as the seventh century.

4. P. Harbison

5. P. Harbison

5. Inishkea North, County Mayo
Ninth/tenth (?) century
Decorated slab

On the small island of Inishkea North, off the western side of the Belmullet Peninsula in County Mayo, an upright slab stands in the sand where it has been exposed to the raw Atlantic winds for well-nigh a thousand years. In contrast to the High Crosses on which the sculpture is usually carved in relief, the figures on the slab are indicated by lightly incised lines. The west face of the slab shown here is dominated entirely by the figure of Christ, its curving features standing out against the largely straight lines of the cross on which he is crucified. Christ's alertly open eyes and his upward-curving mouth give the impression of a triumphant smile, and a possible beard is hinted at by a few vertical lines on the chin. Unlike the majority of earlier Irish crucifixion scenes, this one shows Christ's right as the side pierced by Longinus's spear; on the other side, Stephaton offers Christ vinegar in a hollowed circular vessel on the end of a pole. Both figures are notably smaller than the crucified one. Christ wears a short garment and, beneath it, the upper legs can be seen to bear spiral decoration reminiscent of that on the St. John's Abbey plaque (No. 3). The crosses above the arms may be symbolic of the two thieves or of angels. The slab may conceivably mark the grave of some unknown saint, or it may have been designed to inspire the meditations of those who could have used the spot as one of the stations on their pilgrimage to the holy mountain of Croagh Patrick.

6. Clonmacnois, County Offaly

Tenth century or, more probably, *circa* 1100
Bronze plaque in the National Museum, Dublin

This bronze plaque was found, and probably originally cast, at the famous old monastic site of Clonmacnois on the Shannon. The composition is dominated by the stocky figure of Christ, his head disproportionately large and his bearded face smiling at us over the centuries as he triumphantly conquers death. The nail-head in the palm of each hand invites us to imagine the cross on which he achieves his victory. His body and arms are hidden from us by a long garment stretching to below the knees. It is decorated with half-palmette ornament in stripes that lend force to the horizontal and vertical lines of the cross shape. The contrast is provided by the diagonal lines of Stephaton's pole and Longinus's lance, beneath which the horizontals and verticals are re-established in miniature by the (thieves') crosses, which are neatly placed between the standing figures and the falling sides of Christ's garment. As on many of the earlier High Crosses, Longinus pierces Christ's left (heart) side, and Stephaton offers the vinegar, both figures holding their attributes awkwardly in one hand. Stephaton is the only figure seen in profile; the others are shown frontally, including the two decidedly incorporeal angels—all head, wings, spindly legs, and little body—standing on Christ's arms. The way in which the crucifixion scene dominates its surroundings is emphasized by the overlapping of the decorated frame by Christ's head and hands, as well as by the pole and lance.

6. National Museum of Ireland, Dublin

7. Marrassit or College, County Tyrone

Tenth century or, more probably, *circa* 1100
Bronze plaque from the National Museums of Scotland,
Edinburgh (on loan to the Ulster Museum, Belfast)

Like the previous example, this bronze plaque is between three and four inches high. Here, too, the figures dominate their surroundings by standing out in front of the frame with its finely executed variety of ornament. But there are also marked differences between the two plaques. On this one, the bearded Christ is placed against the background of the cross, to which his hands do not appear to be nailed. The main emphasis is laid, naturally, on Christ himself, for he alone is shown frontally. Longinus pierces Christ's right side, his lance and Stephaton's pole forming the same diagonal contrast with the cross shape as found on the Clonmacnois plaque (No. 6). But here Christ is shown clad in a loincloth, with its hem spreading outward to form a structural link with the garments of the flanking figures. This forms an upward arc that contrasts with the downward arc of Christ's extended arms, drooping languidly as their life-blood ebbs away. The constant interplay of lines, which also links the individual parts of the openwork design to the surrounding frame, is stressed in the hair of Stephaton and Longinus, as well as in the hands, legs, and wings of the angels that fly to the aid of the Savior. It will be noted that the faces of the figures on this and on the Clonmacnois plaque are heavily worn, a feature caused perhaps by the faithful kissing it when it is displayed on Good Friday. The practice of venerating the crucifix in this way continues to our own day, with the Christ figure being cleansed after each kiss.

8. Maghera, County Derry
Third quarter of the twelfth century
Church door lintel

Of the few instances in which a crucifixion scene decorated the lintel over a twelfth-century church doorway, the most expansive is that at Maghera, County Derry, which has been incorporated into the poorly lit interior of a later church tower. Though weathering has caused some erosion of detail in the soft sandstone, we can still clearly make out the figure of Christ in the center, clad in a loincloth and with his inordinately long, thin arms placed against the background of a cross that is much broader than it is high. To the right of it, the half-kneeling Stephaton raises his hyssop-laden vessel on his usual pole; on the left, Longinus also bows his knee as three streams of blood and water pour forth from the wound that his spear has inflicted in Christ's right side. One of the streams, perhaps, falls on his face, as shown on the St. Gall manuscript (No. 1) of some centuries earlier. The two thieves stand unexpectedly on the heads of Stephaton and Longinus respectively, squeezing their bodies between the arms of Christ and the cross, their heads almost touching the wings of the two angels above each arm of the cross. The arms of Christ and the cross were doubtless deliberately lengthened so that the vertical thieves could thereby form subsidiary cross motifs on them. The centurion, standing to the right of Stephaton and raising his sword (?) as he proclaims Christ's divinity, is balanced by an isolated figure on the left, who may represent the Virgin making one of her earliest surviving appearances in an Irish crucifixion scene. But none of the other nine figures witnessing the event can positively be identified, though they probably illustrate pre- and post-crucifixion events. The angels above the arms of the cross are reminiscent of those on the bronze crucifixion plaque from Clonmacnois (No. 6), but the nine peripheral figures are more likely to have been modeled on a crucifixion scene from the European mainland, where they made their first appearance around the beginning of the twelfth century.

8. *Northern Ireland Tourist Board, Belfast*

9. *Dúchas, The Heritage Service, Dublin*

9. Dysert O'Dea, County Clare
Twelfth century
High Cross

The twelfth-century cross at Dysert O'Dea introduces us to a new phase in the representation of the High Cross crucifix image in Ireland, for it is very different from the High Crosses of some centuries earlier (e.g.. Nos. 2 and 4). Gone is the ring, and we no longer have the series of biblical panels decorating the cross (though there are some Old Testament scenes on the base). Instead, we have the long-robed Christ with arms outstretched as he stands out in high relief on the cross-head, resplendent in all his glory—for we behold the triumphant rather than the dead Christ. Christ's head was loose and cemented in more than a century ago, and, if not the original, probably replaces the original head, which may have borne a crown. Beneath Christ is another high-relief figure, wearing a mitre that has been broken off at the top. This figure holds a crosier in the left hand, and its missing right hand—originally pegged in separately—may well have been raised in blessing and may have been in the form of a removable bronze reliquary. The figure is clearly meant to represent an ecclesiastical dignitary, whom some would take to be the hermit Tola, founder of the nearby monastery. Others would identify the figure as a bishop symbolizing new episcopal authority over the old monastery as imposed by twelfth-century church reform. Inscriptions on the base tell us that the cross was repaired in 1683 and again in 1871. But the differing types of ornament on the sides of the upper and lower portions of the cross suggest that the two parts of the cross were not originally carved together as a unit. There can be little doubt, though, that they both emerged at about the same time from a common workshop. Although the Christ and abbot/bishop figure may once have been separated, they still conform to a pattern similar to that present on the Market Cross at Glendalough in County Wicklow. There, a similar configuration is found on the shaft beneath the figure of Christ, who, however, is clad in a loincloth.

10. Tuam, County Galway
1150s
High Cross head

Standing now in the south transept of St. Mary's Protestant Cathedral in Tuam is the Market Cross, which was given that name because it originally stood in the center of the town. It was removed from there to its present position in 1992. This is not a single, uniform cross, but one that is made up of two separate fragments that almost certainly did not belong together originally. The head still retains the ring known from earlier crosses, such as that at Monasterboice (No. 2). This may be partially explained by the notion that the cross to which it belonged was probably commissioned for the royal seat of power by an O Connor king of Connacht, who used the symbol of the ringed cross to signify that his reign should be equated with, and seen as a rival of, the Golden Age of Irish Christian art some three centuries earlier. As at Monasterboice, the ring may represent the cosmos, with the crucifixion as the central event in its history. The figure of Christ is shown in the posture of the crucifixion, though the scene is intended to stress not the suffering of Christ upon the cross but rather his triumph over death and the devil. It is not the crown of thorns but the real crown of a king that Christ bears, to demonstrate his role as *Christus Regnans*—Christ the Triumphant and Christ as Judge. Nevertheless, his head, with its long beard and flowing moustache, falls markedly to the left, suggesting that he is to be understood as dead upon the cross; the two badly worn figures above his head are probably those of ministering angels. The bosses above and below each of his hands are decorations of the cross on which he hangs, and they hint that the cross on which the whole composition was modeled may have been made of bronze, and possibly also of wood. On the model, the figure of Christ would almost certainly have been made of bronze, of the kind seen in the following illustration (No. 11), though in this instance the triangular decoration in Christ's loincloth argues for its having been not Irish but an import from southern England or northern France.

10. P. Harbison

11. The Hunt Museum, Limerick

11. Abbeyderg, County Longford
Late twelfth/early thirteenth century
Bronze figure in the Hunt Museum, Limerick

The Tuam cross-head (No. 10), illustrated on the preceding page, imitates in stone a bronze figure of the kind that was attached to wooden or metal crosses placed on the altars of many churches throughout Europe during the twelfth century. A small number of these bronze figures survive from medieval Ireland, though few attain any high quality of workmanship. Undoubtedly one of the finest examples was found at Red Abbey (Abbeyderg) in County Longford, though its arms and one of the feet sadly have been broken away. The head of Christ is tilted, its diagonal position stressed by the strands of hair that fall vertically onto Christ's right shoulder. A possible crown might indicate that Christ is represented as triumphant, though his closed, lenticular eyes indicate that he is dead. The diagonal ribs are rather schematically shown, but the bronze-founder shows his mastery in the delicate modeling of the folds of the loincloth that flank the central triangular feature, whose sides are more rounded than that of the Tuam cross. The slender elegance of the whole figure stresses all the more the expression of suffering on Christ's face.

12. Donaghmore, County Meath
Twelfth (?) century and later
Round Tower doorway

The Round Towers of Ireland rarely bear any figure sculpture, but the one at Donaghmore, in County Meath, has a rather crude and enigmatic crucifixion above its doorway. Carved in high relief on a horizontal, rectangular stone above the door is the upper part of Christ's body, with outstretched hands; the hand on the left is unfinished. His broad body might suggest that it was intended to show him wearing a long garment. But the lower part of Christ's body on the keystone of the arch beneath is twisted and narrower, creating the suspicion that the two stones, which are of different colors, may not have belonged together originally. Christ's legs are bare and apparently placed one over the other, a feature first seen on the continent around the middle of the twelfth century, but which did not achieve widespread popularity throughout Europe until the thirteenth. The doorjamb is decorated on each side by a head, the one on the left seemingly that of a bare-headed man, the veiled head on the right presumably that of a woman, both in a style scarcely earlier than the thirteenth century. The carving on the stones immediately surrounding the doorway would seem, therefore, to be of a period that is at odds with the pre-1200 date normally ascribed to the Round Towers. Rather than proposing that the Donaghmore tower was built much later than all the others, it is perhaps preferable to suggest that the upper part of the Christ figure belongs to the original building of the tower (in the twelfth century?), and the lower part forms part of a secondary repair to the doorway (thirteenth/fourteenth century), which also included the carving of the two heads. The heads could be those of a husband and wife who commissioned the reconstruction, rather than Mary and St. John, as the Virgin is nearly always on the left, that is, under Christ's right arm.

12. *P. Harbison*

13. Dúchas, The Heritage Service, Dublin

13. Kells, County Meath
Second quarter of the fourteenth century
Tombstone in St. Columba's Church of Ireland

The arrival of the Gothic style in the thirteenth century heralds a marked change in the iconography of the crucifixion. Instead of Christ's two feet being side by side and nailed separately to the cross, they are placed one above the other and pierced with a single nail. This was because new devotions connected with the Arms of Passion (of which the nails formed an important part) came to be associated with the belief that Christ was attached to the cross with a total of only three nails—two for the hands and one for the feet. Stephaton and Longinus are usually omitted, and in their place we generally find the Virgin and St. John. These two figures taken together cannot be identified with any certainty on any Irish crucifixion scenes before the fourteenth century, when they make their earliest surviving appearances in Ireland on a tombstone in the Church of Ireland church in Kells, County Meath. It is also, coincidentally, one of the earliest identifiable uses of a crucifixion on an Irish tombstone. On the bottom of the wedge-shaped stone we find two unidentified Anglo-Norman effigies—a man holding a book and a woman clasping her hands in prayer—and their garments help to date the stone approximately to the second quarter of the fourteenth century. Their feet tread on the foliated tails of a dragon who bites the base of the Tree of Life, which rises between the two effigies and opens out above their heads to act as the ground for the crucifixion scene above. The tree motif is continued in a somewhat different form, not only in the foliage and tree beside the Virgin and St. John, but also in the trefoil terminations of the cross on which Christ hangs. The Tree of Life imagery gained popularity through the Meditations of the Cross of St. Bonaventure, the mid-thirteenth century minister-general of the Franciscans, who described the cross as a tree of leaves and flowers. Christ wears a loincloth with simple folds, and his haloed head, falling to one side in death, is accompanied by two angels carrying censers.

14. Killaspugbrone, County Sligo
Fiacal Phádraig
Circa 1376 and later
National Museum, Dublin

Fiacal Phádraig (St. Patrick's Tooth) is one of the lesser-known Irish shrines of the Middle Ages. It gets its name from the tooth of the national apostle that is said to have fallen on the doorstep of the church of St. Brone in County Sligo, though the shrine was preserved in Cong, County Mayo, until the last century. The oldest part of the shrine probably dates from the twelfth century, but an inscription, part of which is visible here, tells us that the shrine was made for William de Bermingham, Lord of Athenry, perhaps sometime around 1376. The inscription also mentions the names of Sts. Patrick, Brigid, Colmcille, Benan, and Brendan. Though not representing any of these saints, the two figures flanking the crucified Christ probably belong to that part of the shrine commissioned by de Bermingham. Both hold books and appear to be in a seated position, suggesting that they were not designed to form part of a crucifixion group, though they are placed below the arms of a cross with lateral supports (of the kind found on the twelfth-century St. Patrick's Cross on the Rock of Cashel in County Tipperary) and may be part of an Adoration of the Cross scene. But the position of the nails in Christ's hands relative to the background cross could suggest that the Christ figure did not belong to the cross originally and was a subsequent addition, though not necessarily very much later in date. It is a fine piece of Gothic casting, having great strands of hair encircling Christ's head before falling onto his shoulders. His finely modeled and dignified face is bent forward as it tilts to the left, resigned in death. The legs swing out markedly to the left, and he wears a beautifully draped loincloth with diagonal folds. The size of the nail heads seems to be out of all proportion to the Savior's limbs.

14. *National Museum of Ireland, Dublin*

15. *John Kennedy, Green Studio*

15. County Galway
Between 1408 and 1411
The *Leabhar Breac*, page 166
Royal Irish Academy, Dublin

The *Leabhar Breac*, the Speckled Book or, more correctly, the Great Book of Dun Daighre, is one of the great manuscript treasures in the Royal Academy in Dublin. It was written between 1408 and 1411 by a member of the McEgan family on the Galway side of the Shannon, south of Athlone. It contains one of the greatest collections of religious material known from medieval Ireland, most of it collated from very much older monastic sources in the midlands. The text contains narratives and homilies on the birth, life, passion, and resurrection of Our Lord, as well as various versions of the finding of the True Cross in the fourth century. It is appropriate, therefore, that the only representation of the crucified Christ from any later medieval Irish manuscript should be found among its pages. More than any other crucifixion scene from the Irish Middle Ages, it stresses poignantly the suffering of Christ upon the cross. The bearded and haloed head of Christ is burdened by the crown of thorns. The extremely narrow waist at the bottom of the rib-cage impresses upon us how Christ wasted away on the cross in the heat of the Mediterranean sun, his body covered by only a meager loincloth with its ends meeting at the front. We feel the torture when we see the large nails that pierce his feet and hands. It is quite likely that the artist, who was probably not the scribe of the manuscript, used a wooden or bronze crucifix as his model.

16. Holycross, County Tipperary
Circa 1450
Cloister

Holycross Abbey in County Tipperary gets its name from a relic of the True Cross that was presented to it, probably in the twelfth century, and it now has the distinction of having two enshrined fragments of the Cross on display in the church. It is appropriate, therefore, that Holycross is the only medieval Cistercian abbey in Ireland that bears a carving of the crucified Christ in its cloister. The arcade, which was reconstructed some twenty years ago, now gives us an idea of the peaceful atmosphere in which the Irish Cistercians of the Middle Ages would have walked around the cloister. Their prayers would have been inspired by, among other things, the small carved crucifix figure now built into the northeast corner of the cloister. The cross on which Christ hangs is of the simplest variety, having arms of almost equal size, in the Greek manner. Christ's head is tilted noticeably to the left, and his arms are clearly flexed. He wears a simply folded loincloth, above which the abdomen can be seen to be concave. The clear round holes in the hands and feet suggest that the nails may have been inserted in bronze or some other material. Beneath the crucifix is an armorial shield bearing, in its upper right-hand quadrant, the letters IHS for Jesus, with floral patterns emerging from its top and bottom. A short abbot's crosier, with a volute crook of floral design, is carved in false relief at the center of the shield. To the right and left of the crosier is a black-letter inscription, which reads DIONYSIUS O CONGHAIL ABA SCE CRUCIS ME FIERI FECIT (Denis O'Connell, Abbot of Holycross, had me made). On the basis of the occurrence of this name in the Papal Letters, the crucifix may be dated to the years 1448–1455.

16. P. Harbison

17. P. Harbison

17. Crickstown, County Meath
Mid-fifteenth century
Baptismal font, now in Curraha church

It is rare to find the crucifixion represented on baptismal fonts in
Ireland, though the combination need cause us no surprise. The blood
and water that St. John's Gospel tells us issued forth from Christ's
wound were linked by St. Augustine with the sacraments of the church:
blood for the forgiveness of sins and water for baptism. Perhaps the
finest of the Irish examples is on a font from Crickstown, County
Meath, which is now preserved in St. Andrew's Catholic Church at
Curraha. Its donor may have been a member of the Barnewall family,
perhaps Sir Christopher, who was Chief Justice of the King's Bench in
1445–1446. The quality of the workmanship still shines through the
unfortunate coating of whitewash with which the font was covered.
Only the arms of the T-shaped cross, from the ends of which Christ
hangs, are visible. His tall, slender, and beautifully proportioned body
is clad in a seemingly foldless loincloth, the finely-chiseled features of
his youthful and beardless face betraying none of the suffering of the
Leabhar Breac Christ (No. 15), of half a century earlier. To the left we
see the tall figure of the Virgin holding her hands in prayer. She is
balanced on the other side by the graceful St. John who holds a book in
his left hand as he expresses his grief by raising his right hand to his
face. At the corners of the almost-square composition, the evangelist
symbols are shown—the eagle of St. John top left, the standing lion of
St. Mark top right, and the calf of St. Luke in the bottom left. In the
bottom right-hand corner we find St. Matthew writing his gospel,
unusually, in a seated position. Associated with each of the symbols is
an uninscribed scroll, which originally may have borne a painted
inscription. The eight-sided basin of the font also bears carvings of the
Annunciation and of the apostles, some of whom are visible in the
illustration.

18. Ennis Friary, County Clare
Circa 1470
McMahon tomb panel

Built into the Creagh family tomb in the chancel of the old Franciscan Friary in Ennis, County Clare, are panels from an earlier tomb of *circa* 1470, which is traditionally said to have been erected by Máire O'Brien for her husband, Terence McMahon of Corcovaskin, and his family. The crucifixion panel is the most lively example to have survived from medieval Ireland, being filled with a great variety of figures. In the center, Christ hangs from a cross mounted on a pedestal. He has a large halo, but his face has been sadly mutilated by an iconoclast at some period unknown (seventeenth century?). He wears a loincloth with folds on each side. Under each arm of the cross stands an angel holding out a vessel to catch every drop of the precious blood; at the foot of the cross, two further angels kneel as they stretch forth their hands to hold jointly another vessel to catch the blood from the wounds of Christ's crossed feet. Longinus thrusts his spear into Christ's right side, from which no blood emerges. In the bottom left of the panel, the rather squat figure of the Virgin, her cloak held together by a round brooch beneath her chin, is comforted by St. John, who approaches her from the right. Behind her are two further figures who hold the Virgin as she seems to fall backwards in a swoon. On the bottom right we find three soldiers, as well as the long-robed centurion who holds up a scroll bearing an unclear inscription, which probably reads something like "Truly this is the Son of God." The soldiers are clad in the armor of the time (or a little earlier)—aventails or pisanes, and with bascinets on their heads. John Hunt, author of *Irish Medieval Figure Sculpture* (1974), has convincingly suggested that the composition was modeled on an imported English alabaster panel of about 1420–1460, of which a whole set may have been displayed on the high altar of the Friary.

18. P. Harbison

19. Ballymacasey, County Kerry
1479
Processional cross

The most important processional cross to survive from later medieval Ireland was found in fragments during the plowing of reclaimed bogland at Ballymacasey, County Kerry, in 1871. The surviving pieces were later soldered together, though parts of the cross are still missing. It is a silver gilt cross of a type that was common in Europe in the fifteenth century, so that it has few peculiarly Irish characteristics other than the inscription. The gilt figure of Christ hangs down from the cross. Above the rather drawn features of the Savior's face is a rope-like crown encircling the head, from which the hair falls down onto the shoulders. The torso is rather schematically modeled, in contrast to the finely molded folds of the loincloth, the ends of which fall gracefully at the sides. The limbs of the cross are decorated with an openwork acanthus design, and the ends of the arms contain the evangelists' symbols (scarcely visible in the illustration opposite), though the symbol of St. Matthew placed beneath Christ's feet has been lost. A Latin inscription on the arms and upper limb of the cross reads, in translation: "Cornelius, son of John O'Connor, and Eibhlin, daughter of the Knight, caused me to be made at the hands of William Cornelius A.D. 1479." John O'Connor, who founded the nearby Franciscan Friary of Lislaughtin about a decade earlier, died a year before the cross was made: the cross may have been made in his memory.

20. Balrath, County Meath
Later fifteenth century
Wayside cross

Throughout the later Middle Ages it was often the custom to set up a cross on the side of a road, so that the passing traveler could stop and say a prayer for the person who erected it. The most charming—and also one of the earliest surviving examples—of these wayside crosses in Ireland is that on the Dublin-Navan Road opposite the Balrath Post Office. On the side facing away from the road is a touching representation of the crucified Christ. His head is inclined and his hair falls down to his shoulders on both sides. His left arm is raised above his right and his thumbs are flexed. Christ is clad in a flowing loincloth, its upper folds tied into a neat and decorative knot on his right side. His feet, as always in the Gothic period, are placed one above the other, the right foot being vertical and the left one almost horizontal behind it. The knot of interlace above the Savior's head doubtless had a symbolic meaning now lost to us, and the same may also be said of similar motifs elsewhere on the cross. The back of the cross, now facing the road, bears an attractive rendering of the Pietà, a very popular subject in late medieval sculpture. It leads us to reflect upon the sufferings not only of Christ but of his mother as well, as it shows the Virgin grieving for her son, whose body lies across her lap. A rather crude black-letter inscription beneath it asks for a prayer for one Johannes O'Broin, whose name has otherwise disappeared from the pages of history. The presence of the Pietà would suggest a date for the cross in the second half of the fifteenth century, and possibly toward its end. As a further inscription tells us, the cross was later "beautified" by Sir Andrew Aylmer, Baronet, and his wife Catherine, per H. Smith, in the year 1727.

20. P. Harbison

Fresco Paintings in the Abbey of Knockmoy Co Galway on the Monument of O Connor the Founder.

Published by John Jones N.º 90 Bride St Dublin.

21. *After E. Ledwich,* Antiquities of Ireland, *1790*

21. Abbeyknockmoy, County Galway
Fifteenth/sixteenth century
Fresco in church

Many of the medieval churches of Ireland must have had their walls decorated with brightly colored frescoes. But the removal of church roofs and the humidity of the air have reduced the number of remaining frescoes to a mere handful. One of the rare examples known was the crucifixion painted on the chancel wall of the Cistercian Abbey church at Abbeyknockmoy in County Galway. Nothing survives of the fresco today—tragically, for it is the only full fresco crucifixion scene known from the Irish Middle Ages. Fortunately, when more of it was still to be seen, a drawing of it by William Leeson was engraved in Ledwich's *Antiquities of Ireland* of 1790, though we cannot be sure that all his details were correct. It depicts Christ upon the cross, with an uninscribed titulus on the top limb, though we could expect the letters INRI to have been painted on it originally. Christ's body hangs vertically from the cross, and his head tilts sideways. To the left, we see the upper part of a figure with rayed halo, probably to be identified as the Virgin. Opposite it, on the other side, a figure raises its hand as it turns its back to the cross, perhaps representing the centurion. Beneath them, left and right, are two probably female figures, who might represent the two Marys. The whole scene is placed within a Gothic niche, above which there are two larger figures, probably unrelated to the crucifixion, as is another figure further to the right. An inscription indicated the tombs of Maelsechlainn O'Kelly, who died in 1401, and his wife, Finnghuala, who died in 1403, but the relationship of the inscription to the fresco is uncertain. The flourish of the titulus on the top limb of the cross, and the rayed halo of the Virgin, if correctly depicted in Leeson's drawing, might suggest a later date for the fresco, perhaps closer to 1500 (compare to No. 24, of the 1540s).

22. St. Brigid's Cathedral, Kildare
Early sixteenth century
Tomb fragment?

A rectangular limestone slab of uncertain use (architectural or part of a tomb?), now preserved in St. Brigid's Church of Ireland Cathedral in Kildare town, bears an attractive crucifixion scene. It follows the tradition of the Ennis carving of *circa* 1470 (No. 18) in having angels forming a conspicuous part of the whole composition. As at Ennis too, Christ's face is sadly disfigured, but the proportions of the hands and lower legs have become slightly more exaggerated. The projecting left knee lends to the lower part of the body a sense of turning movement, which is heightened by the way in which the flamboyant tubular folds of the loincloth swirl out to the right. On either side of the Savior, an angel in a robe with undulating hem busies itself in collecting the precious drops flowing from Christ's wounds. The angel on the left holds a vessel in each hand, one for the blood from Christ's hand and the other for the blood pouring forth from the side wound; the angel on the right, with prominently fluttering wings, has a single vessel for the spiraling flow from Christ's left hand. Beneath the cross, a third angel looks upward and seems to support the Savior's feet, without holding any visible vessel. One curious feature is the carver's apparent mistake in writing an M instead of an N in the letters decorating the titulus above Christ's tilting head. It lends some support to the theory that the men who carved these stones were not always literate. On the right of the picture, we find the word CENTURIO, referring to an armed figure out of the picture to the right. Beyond that is a carving of the Ecce Homo (not visible here) which, like the Pietà on the Balrath cross (No. 20), serves to call forth our sense of pity for the happenings surrounding Christ's passion and death.

22. P. Harbison

23. *P. Harbison*

23. Fassaroe, County Wicklow

Fifteenth/sixteenth century?
Wayside cross

South Dublin and north Wicklow preserve a small number of crosses, usually of granite, some of which were wayside crosses, as is the case with St. Valery's cross at Fassaroe, County Wicklow, illustrated opposite. They are of simple workmanship, at best folk-carving rather than sculpture. The figure of the crucified Christ is there in all its essential features—the body with arms outstretched—but few details are visible, and the loincloth is scarcely indicated at all. One other cross of this group—that at Kiltuck, County Dublin—was, however, associated with a church and is now re-erected in the grounds of the Catholic church at Shankill. It supplies one important detail that is unclear on the Fassaroe cross, namely the feet of Christ crossed in an X. This helps us to date these crosses firmly at the end of the Middle Ages, rather than to the Romanesque period in the twelfth century to which they have hitherto been assigned. The beveled, chamfered edges of the crosses, particularly noticeable at Kiltuck and on a fragmentary cross-head recently re-erected at the center of Blackrock village, would argue for a date toward the end of the Gothic period, or even later. Despite their naiveté, these crosses are witnesses of a strong faith that led people to erect them without getting either credit or prayers for having done so, as there is no trace of any inscription (although perhaps one was painted on originally and obliterated by the rains of centuries). There is a curious boss (originally a face?) on the base of the Fassaroe cross, but what its purpose was is unknown.

24. Great Connell, County Kildare

Circa 1540–1550
Tomb of Bishop Wellesley now in St. Brigid's
Cathedral, Kildare

In 1971, a number of medieval tomb-surrounds were removed from
the churchyard wall at Great Connell and brought to St. Brigid's
Cathedral in Kildare town, where they were assembled together to support the fine effigy of Bishop Walter Wellesley (d. 1539), which had
been brought from Great Connell at the same time. One of these is the
crucifixion panel reproduced here, which was created by one of the
three or more sculptors who are thought to have worked on the bishop's
tomb not long after his death. Its features bear a certain nobility that
betrays the initial stages of Renaissance influence on Irish carving.
Christ hangs on a cross that is topped by a scroll rolled up at both ends
and bearing the letters INRI. What strikes the beholder most about
Christ is the resigned, yet almost beatific, look on his face, far removed
from the tortured features on the *Leabhar Breac* crucifixion (No. 15) of
a century and a quarter earlier. The smiling countenance is shared by
the book-holding figure of St. John to the right of the cross. Both he
and the Virgin, to the left of the cross, have an ornamental, petalled
halo. The Virgin, though, has a more earnest and transcendental mien
than the other two figures, giving the impression that her thoughts are
far away and that she is contemplating the sadness of the scene she has
to witness.

24. D. H. Davison/Irish Picture Library

25. St. Canice's Cathedral, Kilkenny
1552
Tomb of John Grace

St. Canice's Church of Ireland Cathedral in Kilkenny houses what is probably the most extensive collection of medieval tomb-sculpture in the country, showing the city to have been an important center for the stone carver's art. Through inscriptions, we know the O'Tunney family formed one of the important workshops active in the area. The most notable member of the family was Rory, who signed his name to the effigy of John Grace, dating from 1552. Beneath its western end is a crucifixion scene that probably belonged to the tomb originally. It shows Christ hanging from a cross with square terminals to the arms, and foliate quatrefoils above. Christ's loincloth extends outward with a flourish on both sides. The body musculature is somewhat schematized, and he wears a richly curling beard. On the left is the Virgin, with hands folded in prayer and an attractive veil falling down over her arms. On the other side is St. John with a fine wavy coiffure. He is holding a rolled-up scroll in one hand. The most noticeable characteristic is how, by the middle of the sixteenth century, there is a tendency for the figures to be much more squat, in contrast to the finely proportioned figures of the Great Connell crucifixion (No. 24), carved less than two decades earlier. Above, we can see the decorative lettering with which Rory O'Tunney signed his name: RORICUS O TWNNE FABRICAVIT ISTAM [TUMBAM] (Rory O'Tunney made this [tomb]).

26. Johnstown, County Kilkenny
Later sixteenth century
Stone crucifix

Built into the north wall of the forecourt leading up to the Catholic church in Johnstown is an intensely dramatic crucifixion, which may have been brought here from the nearby church at Fertagh. Its original function there, however, remains unknown. Christ's curiously proportioned body is placed against a limestone cross of equal size that follows the twist of the lower part of Christ's body by turning to the left as it descends. His face bears a look of poignant suffering, heightened by the disfigurement of the carving caused by the removal of the nose, which may have been inserted secondarily after the original nose was broken. The arms are shown in a very schematic, faceted style, foreshadowing some of the sculpture of our own century. The high collarbone and the tubular ribs, as well as the empty, triangular abdomen, call forth our sympathy for the way in which the Savior has become "skin and bone" on the cross. The faceted legs and feet are double-crossed and twisted in torment, an effect achieved by the unrealistic shortening of the Savior's left leg. The straight lines of the upper part of Christ's body form a contrast to the flowing curves of the loincloth, which is tucked up neatly into a knot to the right of his waist. The cross is difficult to date. The positioning of the legs and feet hark back to earlier styles of the fifteenth century, but the flamboyant loincloth and the rugged carving of Christ's face suggest a date scarcely earlier than the sixteenth century, and probably not before its second half.

26. P. Harbison

27. P. Harbison

27. Kilmore, County Meath
1575
Tombstone of Rory Buí McMahon

Lying flat outside the south wall of the medieval church at Kilmore, County Meath, is the tombstone of the scribe Rory Buí McMahon. The outline of the elongated Latin cross is clearly visible, against which the simplified form of the crucified Christ is placed asymmetrically, with outspread and rather cadaverous legs, and the head tilted to one side. The sculptor hides his lack of craftsmanship by reducing the body and legs to simple swelling and contracting forms, demonstrating at the same time the low ebb that Irish figure sculpture had reached during the period of the Elizabethan wars. It is obvious that the sculptor was more at home in carving the letters of the long inscription in high false relief. The tombstone is of interest not only in giving us an exact date of 1575, placed under Christ's left arm, but also in the use of both Irish and Latin in the inscriptions, which are only partially visible in the illustration opposite. The Latin inscription, in English lettering on the left, reads in translation: "No one ought to be grieved at death, since in living there is labor and danger, while in dying there is peace and the assurance of resurrection. Pray for the soul of Rory McMahon who had me made." The Irish inscription, in Irish lettering, on the right of the picture, states the following, also in translation: "God expects from everyone who reads this, and understands that the pains of purgatory are the shorter and the mercy of God the more speedy for the prayers of Christians, to offer a prayer of charity for the soul of him who wrote this, and for whom it was written, namely Rory Buí McMahon."

28. St. Brigid's Cathedral, Kildare
Circa 1621
Tomb chest of Walter Walsh

One of the most unusually decorative of all the Irish crucifixion scenes is found on a rectangular block of stone preserved in St. Brigid's Church of Ireland Cathedral in Kildare. The upper parts of the cross consist largely of rigid patterns, with a flowing scroll bearing the letters INRI on top. Christ hangs slightly from the cross. His bearded face bears the grimace of the sufferer, and the prickly crown of thorns hangs heavily upon his haloed head. Blood flows clearly from the wound in his side, and he wears a neatly patterned loincloth. Particular emphasis is laid on the nails in his hands and feet, the fingers of his right hand clenching under the pressure. Beside the cross stand two stylishly orna-mental figures, with hair and clothes reminiscent of the Elizabethan style. The figure on the left has the hands folded on the breast; that on the right has them placed side by side. The two haloed figures are so similar that it is difficult to know whether they represent the Virgin and St. John or two female figures. All of the figures are placed against the strongly patterned background of foliage that dominates the compo-sition. From it, a small cross falls above Christ's right arm, and among the leaves on either side of Christ's body there is something which resembles a chalice, presumably to hold the blood. The stone served as the end-panel of the tomb of Walter Walsh, a dean of Kildare who died in 1621, and one gets the impression that the carving could be a con-temporary woodcut.

28. P. Harbison

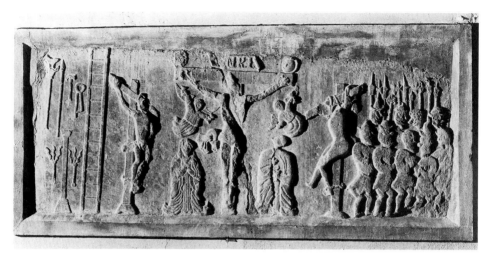

29. P. Harbison

29. St. Multose Church, Kinsale, County Cork

First half (?) of seventeenth century
Tomb-front or reredos

After the Ennis carving of *circa* 1470 (No. 18), perhaps the most vividly crowded and iconographically rich of all the Irish crucifixion scenes is that on a stone found earlier this century in the Galwey Chapel of St. Multose church in Kinsale, and now built into the interior south aisle. Sadly, the stone is broken in the middle, causing considerable damage to the crucified Christ at the center of the composition. The sun and moon make their appearance above the ends of the arms, flanking the titular scroll bearing the letters INRI. As at Ennis, angels hover beneath Christ's arms to catch the precious blood flowing from the nail-wounds and from his side. Mary, with a detached look, is shown frontally beneath the angel on the left; St. John, who balances her on the right, holds his chalice and participates more directly in the tragic happening by looking up at the Savior on the cross. The figures of the two thieves are bound to their own crosses, which are carved, unexpectedly, in perspective. On the left of the scene are some of the instruments of the Passion, which had already begun to make their appearance on Irish tombstones as early as the fifteenth century—the pillar and the scourge used in the flagellation, and the ladder, spear, hammer, and pincers used in the crucifixion. On the right-hand end of the slab, a crowd of soldiers adds tremendous animation to the scene, as they hold up their lethal collection of pikes. Some of their faces are grotesque caricatures, reminiscent of a seventeenth-century Dutch painting—an echo which is perhaps not unintentional, for Kinsale was a port that was often in closer contact with far distant parts than it was with the rest of Ireland.

30. and 31. Kilmacduagh, County Galway
Seventeenth century
Tomb panels

The seventeenth century produced a number of carved stone crucifixion scenes that may be described as a charming expression of ornamental folk art. Two examples are chosen for illustration opposite. Both are in a side chapel of the Cathedral at Kilmacduagh, the upper one carved in the first half of the century, the lower one dating probably from the second half. The earlier example shows Christ with an outsized head, charmingly bearded and wearing a brief V-shaped loincloth curling up into a lovely little roll on one side. Beside him are the Virgin and St. John. They are almost identical bottle-shaped figures with no feet. The only distinguishing feature is that the Virgin, on the left, folds her hands across her breast. The letters INRI above the cross are included in a Latin inscription, in raised English lettering, which runs around three sides of the panel. It contains a prayer asking that God be above us and hailing the Virgin with the request that she have mercy upon us. The later plaque has a more corporeal Christ, whose chest muscles are realistically attempted. He wears an interwoven crown of thorns and a short loincloth that curls around itself in an ornamental fashion to the right. Its accompanying Virgin and St. John are clad similarly with long, splaying garments, their shoulders covered with a cloak that opens down the front. Both figures clasp their hands in prayer, with the Virgin facing to the front and St. John seen in half profile. Note-worthy is what must surely be taken to be a curly wig on St. John's head. These two plaques presumably formed the end panels of tombs carved, probably, some decades apart.

30. and 31. P. Harbison

32. P. Harbison

32. Athcarne, County Meath
Mid-seventeenth century
The White Cross

One of the few pieces of real sculpture, as opposed to just stone-carving, found among the crucifixions of the seventeenth century is that on the wayside cross at Athcarne, County Meath, known as the White Cross. Its creator has risen high above the level of folk art so typical of this period (Nos. 30–31 and 33), and has managed to impart a sense of happy yet mortal resignation to Christ's strong face, while imbuing the body with a feeling for sculpture in the round. The sculptor penetrates the skin to show the ribcage and the undulating musculature beneath, while the legs are those of a powerful athlete. Christ's feet are placed side by side, a feature unusual at this period, and one that harks back to the pre-Gothic era. Beneath them is a skull, illustrating the old tradition that Adam was buried at the spot where Christ's cross was erected on Golgotha, which Christians took to be the center of the world. The brief and flowing loincloth, like the short arms of the cross, presents a horizontal axis that contrasts with the vertical line of Christ's body and arms. The striking composition of the Christ with his arms raised upright on the cross is a true break-away from the normal Irish style of the time. Apparently, it is based on a model pioneered by Rubens and later practiced by the continental sculptors of the 1630s, who were influential in the development of the Baroque style in Germany. It is difficult to know, therefore, whether the incised inscription of circa 1665 naming Dame Cecilie Bath on the side of the cross is contemporary or a later addition. The decoration on the base (not shown here) and the rather top-heavy cap of the cross would not argue against a date in the 1660s, so that the sculptor may have been using a foreign model already thirty years old when he carved the figure of Christ. The other side of the cross bears an attractive representation of the Virgin and Child, accompanied by heraldic devices and instruments of the Passion.

33. Ballyhaunis, County Mayo
Seventeenth/eighteenth century
Wooden crucifix figure in the Augustinian friary

The churches of medieval and early modern Ireland, which we now see as ruined ghosts in the landscape, must have had their share of religious furnishings that have now almost entirely disappeared. Many of the wooden statues that may have originally adorned them probably fell prey to woodworm or the hand of the iconoclast. One of the rare survivors would appear to be a wooden crucifix figure preserved in the Augustinian Friary at Ballyhaunis in County Mayo, which was discovered in 1908 in the O'Gara altar of 1739 in the old friary church. The arms of Christ are a later replacement and, although the cross to which they are nailed is unashamedly modern, the head, torso, and legs of the Christ figure look original. Christ's beardless head is tilted to one side, and his lenticular eyes are closed in death. His slightly S-curving body shows a semblance of muscular modeling, as do the knees and calves of the legs, but the ribcage above the contracted abdomen is indicated merely by lightly incised grooves in the outer surface of the skin. The loincloth consists of a few sparse horizontal folds of cloth that combine into a knot before falling in a fan-shaped flurry at Christ's left thigh. The Savior's rather stocky legs and feet are placed side by side, a feature that—along with strands of hair falling down onto the right shoulder—may well be an echo of some Romanesque crucifix (e.g. No. 11) preserved in the country. But the taut and skimpy horizontal folds of the loincloth are comparable to those on some stone examples preserved in the friary grounds, and to others in Connacht datable to the seventeenth century. The juxtaposed feet and the muscular modeling, found in a more refined form in the Athcarne Cross (No. 32), could also be seen to suggest for the Ballyhaunis figure a seventeenth- or early eighteenth-century stage of development, before wood-carving declined in quality toward the primitive folk art found in the later crucifixes of the Penal Crosses (No. 38).

33. P. Harbison

34. P. Harbison

34. Cruicetown, County Meath
1688
Cruise/Dalton Cross

After the sculptural heights reached at Athcarne (No. 32), the crucifixion on the cross in Cruicetown churchyard, also in County Meath, reverts more to the level of folk art. Yet, the cross is not without its interesting features. The inscription, which starts on the other face and runs onto the one that is illustrated opposite, asks us to pray for the souls of Patrick Cruise and Catherine Dalton, his wife, daughter of William and Elizabeth Dalton of Miltown, who had the cross made in 1688. At the time, James II had been on the throne for only three years, but already the majority Catholic population in Ireland had come to expect him to relax religious oppression and to allow them to return to the practice of the religion of their forefathers. It is not without significance, therefore, that during the course of the same year, 1688, a centuries-old market cross, with its Celtic ring, was re-erected in the town of Kells, not far away—an act of political symbolism reviving the greatness of the Golden Age of Irish Christianity a millennium earlier. Because it is unusual at this period, the ring around the head of the Cruicetown cross ought similarly to be seen as echoing the desire for the revival of the Celtic past under a Stuart king. But, as we know, it was a very short-lived Celtic revival, for William of Orange was waiting in the wings, and the battle fought out on the Boyne nearby only two years later was to bring those Catholic hopes to an all-too-abrupt end. On this cross, the body of Christ stands out in sunken relief, as does also Adam's skull beneath it. Christ's head tilts to the right in death, his hair surrounded by the crown of thorns, and his torso formed of a very chunky block of stone, lacking the rippling musculature of the Athcarne cross. Above the usual letters INRI is a very serious winged angel.

35. Mainham, County Kildare
1743
Altar frontal of the Browne mausoleum

During the eighteenth century, Ireland was ruled by a minority Protestant ascendancy that repudiated representations of religious subjects, including crucifixions, as they smacked too much of popery. It is all the more surprising, therefore, to find two members of the aristocracy, dressed in all the finery of the period, represented as kneeling on cushioned stools before a crucifix on the altar-front of the Browne mausoleum at Mainham, dating from 1743. But the explanation is that the pair, identified by initials as Stephen Browne (of nearby Castle Browne, now Clongowes Wood) and his wife, Judith Browne, alias Wogan, both came from among those rare landowning families that remained true to the Catholic faith throughout the penal days. Reading between the lines of an inscription above the door of the mausoleum leads one to presume that it was because of his religion that Browne was denied permission by the Protestant Rector of Clane to erect his burial monument inside the grounds of the old church at Mainham. Instead, he erected a mausoleum on his own land immediately outside the churchyard wall. The carving can be seen, therefore, as a symbol of Catholic defiance against the established Church, a gesture further emphasized in the depiction of Stephen removing his three-cornered hat in the presence of the crucifix, and Judith clasping rosary beads, of which this must be one of the earliest Irish illustrations. Judith, who was buried here in 1746, and Stephen, who did not die until 1767, are the ancestors of the Wogan-Browne family.

35. P. Harbison

36. P. Harbison

36. Seir Kieran, County Offaly
Circa 1790
Brooder tombstone

During the penal times of the eighteenth century, the Catholic majority were actively discouraged from displaying religious works of art, which their impoverishment could not have paid for anyway. But with the increasing tolerance of the late eighteenth century, some of those who could afford it were able, at least in death, to give visual expression of their faith by reviving their earlier practice of erecting tombstones decorated with the crucifixion. Many of the scenes were carved with the compelling and naïve charm of a folk art beginning to reestablish itself after decades of suppression. These tombstones are numerous in the eastern part of the country, but the Brooder family headstone chosen for illustration here comes from Seir Kieran in the south midlands, where it was erected probably around 1790. It may have been carved by the celebrated stonecutter Denis Cullen of Monaseed. The large figure of the crucified Christ dominates the scene in the upper third of the stone. The smaller figure of Longinus reappears, dressed in contemporary costume as he pierces Christ's side with a lance. On the opposite side, the even smaller centurion surveys the scene on horseback. The remaining space is filled out with the instruments of the Passion—the ladder, nail, and pincers, as well as the hammer on the centurion's side; Longinus is surrounded by the scourge of flagellation. Behind his head is an illustration of the medieval legend of the cock and the pot. The dice can be seen above the arms of the cross, and the thirty pieces of silver are laid out horizontally beneath the whole scene.

37. Navan, County Meath

1792

Crucifix figure by Edward Smyth in the Catholic parish church

Edward Smyth has gone down in the annals of Irish art as the sculptor of the riverine heads of Dublin's Custom House and of other important architectural ornaments on many of the capital's Georgian buildings. Unique among his *oeuvre*, and his only purely religious carving, is a crucifix in the Catholic church in Navan, which may be his native place. He may have stemmed from a family of sculptors, for it has been speculated that he may have been related to the H. Smith who was instrumental in "beautifying" the nearby wayside cross at Balrath (No. 20) in 1727. This wooden crucifix may be the earliest known Irish example to which the sculptor has appended his name. Unexpectedly large in size, it is a piece of sculpture even more remarkable than that of the Christ figure on the Athcarne cross (No. 32) in the same county. The flamboyant loincloth reveals a very Baroque flourish in style when compared to the neoclassical fashion in vogue at the time. But the modeling of the powerful musculature of the torso is a fine academic essay in the best tradition of Greek and Roman sculpture. The head of Christ is invested with a noble sense of dignity, the lips showing a disdain for the torment that he had suffered before he closed his eyes in death. Small details, such as the curving up of the fingers, make us realize what tremendous symbolism Smyth has brought into the execution of this figure, which fortunately lacks any of the sentimentality that Italian influence was to bring into the carving of such figures in the following century.

37. *National Gallery of Ireland*

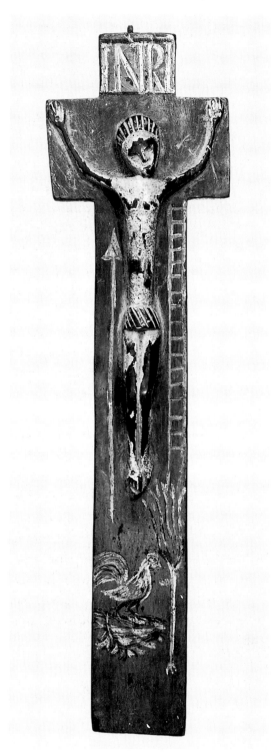

*38. National Museum of Ireland, Dublin, by courtesy of
the President of University College, Galway*

38. County Galway (?)
1797
Penal cross in University College, Galway

No greater contrast can be imagined than that provided by the comparison of the nobility of the Edward Smyth crucifix in Navan (No. 37) with the formalized rigidity of the so-called Penal Crosses. After the solitary peak achieved by Smyth, we descend here into the valleys of a folk art, often awkward in its execution, yet, in its popularity, expressive of the deep religious feelings of the many who bought them. These Penal Crosses got their not-always-justified name from the fact that they were first carved during the penal days of the eighteenth century, though the tradition of carving them continued into the more tolerant years of the nineteenth. A.T. Lucas, who wrote a book on Penal Crosses forty years ago, has argued plausibly for connecting their creation with the pilgrimage made to St. Patrick's Purgatory in Lough Derg, County Donegal. Penal Crosses are usually made of wood and, as does the crucifix figure, they generally bear a selection of the instruments of the Passion. The penal cross illustrated here, which is preserved in University College, Galway, is one of the better-quality examples, displaying the characteristics typical of the genre. On the front, we see the elongated and stylized figure of Christ standing out in high relief, wearing a brief, hatched loincloth, and with his head decorated with a rayed halo. In addition to the incised letters INRI at the top of the cross, we find the ladder, lance, and scourge of the Passion, as well as a realistically drawn cock. Because it is lacking the pot that often accompanies it, the cock can be taken as that which crowed three times when Peter denied Christ. The back of the cross is incised with the letters IHS and the date 1797.

39. Termonfechin, County Louth
1818
Tombstone of Edward Rodgers

40. Monasterboice, County Louth
1801
Tombstone of James Murphy

County Louth preserves a series of fine tombstones from around 1800 that bear charming carvings of the crucifixion and some of the scenes leading up to it. Two of these are illustrated opposite. The tombstone of Edward Rodgers at Termonfechin shows Christ carrying his cross to Calvary. The figure of the Savior is bent forward under the strain of bearing his enormous cross, as he is nobly assisted in the task by Simon of Cyrene. On the right, Veronica holds the cloth she offered to Christ to dry his face, and which henceforth bore his countenance. The scene is framed at either end by a soldier carrying a spear and extending an arm to point out to Christ the way to Calvary. The tombstone of James Murphy at Monasterboice, some seventeen years earlier, brings us closer to the moment of the crucifixion, as it shows Christ being raised on the cross. Here we have the cross in the process of being erected, with Christ already nailed to it. The stiff figure of the Savior, with its simplified loincloth and rayed head, bears an obvious similarity to the representations of Christ on the Penal Crosses (e.g., No. 38). We are drawn into the scene by observing the strenuous labor involved in erecting the cross, with one man pushing one of its arms and another raising it with his back, while two more men pull at a rope tied to the other arm of the cross. Longinus looks on, holding his spear on the left; the centurion appears on horseback from the right, as he does also on the Seir Kieran tombstone (No. 36). Angels, all wings and head but no body, hover above the scene like birds. Beneath are the words that the Emperor Constantine saw in his dream: IN HOC SIGNO VINCES (In this sign you will triumph).

39. and 40. P. Harbison

41. P. Harbison

41. Glasnevin Cemetery, Dublin

1862
Memorial to Dr. Alexander MacDonnell

In the wake of the Catholic Emancipation Act of 1829, the conscious desire to demonstrate the unbroken religious tradition in Ireland from the period before the Reformation was forcefully expressed in the erection of hundreds of churches imitating the Gothic style of the fifteenth-century abbeys and friaries. Their ruinous stone shells were a constant reminder of the oppression of the intervening years. But the moveable furnishings of these medieval churches, being of less durable materials, had in comparison scarcely survived at all to provide appropriate models for the interior fittings of the nineteenth-century churches. In their absence, stereotype crucifixes and Stations of the Cross were introduced from Italy, usually exuding a sentimental pathos and having an artistic standard that rarely rose above the pedestrian. Yet, the nineteenth century saw not only the revitalization of the Gothic but also the revival of interest in the even older Celtic past, embodied in the rising popularity of the use of the ringed Celtic cross in the host of tombstones dating from the second half of the century. One of the most interesting of these is the memorial to Dr. Alexander MacDonnell, who was buried in Glasnevin Cemetery in 1862. It copies the style of thousand-year-old crosses (e.g., No. 2) not only in its interlace ornament, but also in the way one face of the shaft is decorated with narrative scenes (not shown here). They illustrate not the Bible, as on the earlier crosses, but the corporal works of mercy—as befitted the work of a philanthropic doctor. At the center of the west face, Christ is shown crucified on a ringed cross that has shamrock sprouting on its upper limb. The cross thereby becomes the Tree of Life, topped by a nest with the pelican—symbolizing the Church— feeding its young with the blood flowing from its breast, which it pierces with its beak. The ends of the arms of the larger ringed cross feature the lively symbols of the four evangelists bearing the scrolls of their respective Gospels.

42. Glasnevin Cemetery, Dublin
1875
Memorial to Thomas Joseph Ryan

Nineteenth-century Irish tastes considered crucifixes and crucifixions suitable not only for church interiors but also for the tombstones of the more affluent members of the rising middle classes, as we have already seen in the memorial to Dr. MacDonnell in Glasnevin (No. 41). Having been the national cemetery for the last one hundred and fifty years, Glasnevin offers us a better selection of high quality Victorian Catholic tombstones than anywhere else in the country. These include some fine representations of the crucifixion, though some betray the pedestrian emptiness of the Victorian period. One of the better examples is the monument to Thomas Joseph Ryan, of 1875. It is entirely in keeping for a man who died at the tragically young age of twenty-five that a poignant note should be struck in the carving above his tomb. It portrays in a very realistic fashion the sadness of the scene on Calvary. On the left, with her hands folded in prayer, the Virgin stands grieving for her son, the desolation on her face a visual expression of that inspiring hymn "Stabat Mater Dolorosa." Opposite her, St. John, holding his Gospel in one hand, strikes a dignified pose as he places the other hand on his breast. He looks more directly at the stark outline of the cross bearing the figure of the crucified Christ, the simple folds of whose loincloth act as a foil to the much richer drapery of the garments worn by the flanking figures. The realism of the scene is underlined by the three wedges used to anchor the cross on the pedestal carved in the shape of natural rock. We are thereby mentally transported to the rock of Golgotha, the physical location of the crucifixion where medieval legend also placed the tomb of Adam, whose skull and bones are prominently displayed beneath the cross. The rock formation continues down into the base, which is naturalistically decorated with ivy, a fern, and a flowering branch.

42. P. Harbison

43. P. Harbison

43. Séamus Murphy: The Twelfth Station of the Cross
1935
White marble panel (private collection)

The Corkman Séamus Murphy (1907–1975) is one of the most loved and revered of Ireland's twentieth-century stone carvers—a man who fused the talents of craftsman and artist into one harmonious whole, and whose book *Stone Mad* gives us one of those rare literary illuminations of a trade so amusingly described by one of its own best practitioners. The country's finest portrait sculptor, he is also rightly famed for his distinctive hand-cut lettering, which stands out so conspicuously from the machine-made product. His religious works are not numerous, and apparently the only crucifixion scene he ever executed is a Twelfth Station of the Cross, completed early on in his career. Sensitively carved in clear white marble, and signed SM in the bottom right-hand corner, this panel represents a new approach and a welcome breakaway from the dull plaster Stations that filled the walls of so many Irish churches of the nineteenth and early twentieth centuries. The carefully composed groupings of the figures around the foot of the cross show the success of his academic training, so recently completed at the time. The beautifully modeled heads of the three Marys (with their jar of ointment) on the right are attractively arranged at different angles, and the sense of depth created by the massing of the figures one behind the other is delicately emphasized by the gently curving outlines of their cloaks. Their demure and noble pathos is shared by the figure of the Virgin to the left of the cross, whose hands partially cover her face in grief. She is grouped with St. John and the centurion with his upright lance, while the Magdalene embraces the feet of the cross-nimbed Savior, whose lifeless body forms the centerpiece of the whole composition. The quality of this solitary Station demonstrates how much greater Séamus Murphy's contribution to Irish religious art of the twentieth century would have been had he persevered in completing the other thirteen Stations of the set.

44. St. Joseph's Church, Terenure, Dublin

1920 Harry Clarke's stained-glass windows:
The Crucifixion and *The Adoration of the Cross*

Of all the stained-glass artists who have graced the Irish scene in the twentieth century, the most imaginative and exciting is surely Harry Clarke (1889–1931). When he died at the tragically young age of forty-one, his work had achieved a beauty in both color and design that bid fair to rival Chartres. No reproduction can convey his indescribably brilliant deep blues, purples, and reds. His figures' bejeweled garments and ornamental backgrounds are decorated in minute detail worthy of the Book of Kells. Encomiums of praise were rightly heaped upon his *Adoration of the Cross* when it was unveiled to the public in St. Joseph's Church, Terenure, in 1920 (though its position in the church has since been altered). The three vertical lights together are horizontally divided into three sections, an earth below, a heaven above, and, between them, a twilight zone of trees beneath the dome of an orange sky, darkly glowing with the sun and moon at the hour of the crucifixion. The slender Christ, with cross-nimbed head and upright arms, hangs on a tall, thin, studded, brown cross that soars upward like a Jacob's ladder uniting earth with heaven, where the choir of angels frame the Holy Spirit in the form of a dove. Despite the crown of thorns, we have here a return to the old, pre-Gothic Christ Triumphant with juxtaposed feet which, together with the raised arms, are strongly reminiscent of the Christ at Athcarne (No. 32). Isolated at the foot of the cross is an artistically arranged emotive trio: the Virgin and St. John, standing with their heads bowed in grief as their hands fold in silent prayer, and beneath them the golden-haired Magdalene—the most ravishing figure of the window—dressed in a patterned cloak of wondrous blue, as she kneels in meditation on the death of her Savior. The whole magnificent composition is rounded off by groups of male and female Irish saints venerating the cross in the earthly part of the two side lights.

The stained glass window contains the following inscriptions:

ORA PRO ANIMABUS
ELIZABETH et JOANNAE
deVERDON CORCORAN

AD·MAJOREM
DEI·GLORIAM

ORA PRO·ANIMA
LAURENTII·GORMAN
DONATORIS·R·I·E

44. Michael Blake

45. *Paddy Tutty, reproduced by courtesy of the Hugh Lane Municipal Gallery of Modern Art, Dublin, and Professor Michael Purser (as representative of the heirs and successors of Mainie Jellett)*

45. Dublin: The Hugh Lane Municipal Gallery of Modern Art
1941
Mainie Jellett's oil painting, *The Ninth Hour*

The twentieth century has seen the emergence of women as major contributors to the development of religious art in Ireland, and Mainie Jellett (1867–1944) ought to be counted as one of the most significant among them. She studied in Paris in the 1920s, where her teachers, Lhote and Gleizes, gave her a firm grounding in the principles of cubism, which she saw as a reaction to the materialism of the nineteenth century. She introduced the new style into Ireland in 1924, gradually developing and adapting it to suit her own subject matter. Her work includes a crucifixion that she painted in oils on a panel, entitled *The Ninth Hour*, now in the Municipal Gallery, Dublin. She depicts the haloed Christ with outstretched arms on the cross, his torso shown frontally but with his legs largely in profile. He is flanked by the realistically painted thieves who languish on crosses that recede in a perspective reminiscent of that seen on the Kinsale stone (No. 29). Beneath the cross we see the Virgin on the left and St. John on the right, both with their hands clasped in prayer. The figure of the Magdalene is seen on the bottom left, and the crested helmet of the centurion on the bottom right. The remainder of the panel is occupied by a harmonious color composition of graceful curves and geometric forms. The canvas embodies the artist's own idea of seeking "the inner principle and not the outward appearance," and fulfills her aim "to search for the inner rhythms and constructions of natural forms; to create on their pattern; to make a work of art a natural creation complete in itself, based on the eternal laws of balanced harmony and ordered movement." The crucifixion panel should, as she said, "be looked at, first as a harmony of color and form, apart from any realistic story-telling idea.... The picture is... like a small universe, controlled by a defined rhythmic movement within a given space. It is akin to the old Celtic tradition." With her revival of the early Irish love of abstract ornament (e.g., No. 3), the old Celtic wheel can truly be said to have come full circle with Mainie Jellett.

46. Kingscourt, County Cavan
1947–48
Stained-glass window by Evie Hone in the Catholic church

Evie Hone (1894–1955) belonged to a family that has given Ireland a number of noted artists throughout the last two centuries. After studying in London, she went to Paris in the early 1920s and there met Mainie Jellett (No. 45), who was to become her lifelong friend. But she turned away from the secular world of Parisian art, and after a short spell as an Anglican nun in Cornwall, she returned to Ireland where she was received into the Catholic church in 1937. A person of deep religious conviction, she became—with Harry Clarke (No. 44)—one of the most outstanding Christian artists of her generation in Ireland and, indeed, in Europe. She produced a wide range of works in stained glass, a medium she first practiced in 1933, and which she was to make her own for the rest of her life. She toured widely in Ireland, sketching a number of old stone carvings that, along with the art of Rouault, were to find echoes in her subsequent work. She created a number of crucifixions, the best known of which is her eighteen-light window in Eton College Chapel. Smaller in scale, but nonetheless very attractive in its conception, is the two-light crucifixion that she executed for the nave of the Catholic church in Kingscourt, County Cavan. There it is flanked by an Annunciation scene, as well as an Ascension that is considered to be one of the greatest stained-glass windows in Ireland. The right-hand light of the crucifixion shows Christ hanging almost vertically on the cross, his hands raised in a pose so similar to that of the Athcarne cross (No. 32) that one may well ask if it was not a model for this composition. The white hue of his simple loincloth and the pink tones of the Savior's skin contrast with the deep rich blue of the sober garment of the Virgin, who is seen kneeling with her hands in prayer at the bottom of the left-hand light. Above her is a neat grouping of the three Marys, and behind them the landscape recedes into the distance, where it is dominated by what looks like a small Irish country cottage.

46. *P. Harbison*

47. P. Harbison

47. Cookstown, County Tyrone

1964
Stained-glass window by Patrick Pye in
the Convent of Mercy

As stained glass is undoubtedly one of Ireland's greatest contributions to modern art, no apology need be made here for the inclusion of yet a third stained-glass window of the crucifixion. This one, the work of Patrick Pye, illuminates the chapel of the Convent of Mercy in Cookstown, County Tyrone. Pye was born in England in 1929 but was educated in Ireland, studying under Oisín Kelly and John Murphy in Dublin, and Albert Troost at Maastricht in Holland. He has developed his own very individual style in a variety of media, including etching and oil painting. As Pye is an artist of religious conviction, it is not surprising that stained glass features among his best-known work; his windows can be seen in Glenstal Abbey and in Westport, County Mayo, among other places. Because his crucifixion scene in Cookstown is in a convent, it is one of his less frequently seen works, but one which expresses a variety of moods in the contrast between the darker colors in the upper half and the lighter colors below. The darkest part of the whole window is, in fact, the figure of Christ, which seems to brood with a sense almost of despair more than suffering, as if contemplating the evils of the world. Yet the slanting leaded lines coming down diagonally from the left seem to bring rays of hope from heaven, as they brighten up the cross. We are reminded of the thieves by the presence of two figureless crosses flanking Christ; St. John the Evangelist and the Blessed Virgin wait mutely at the foot of the cross. One of the most notable and brightest figures of the panel is the centurion, who views the scene from horseback, as on the folk art stones of the eighteenth and nineteenth centuries (Nos. 36 and 40). Longinus is reintroduced but, unusually, he pierces Christ's right side from horseback also, his mount being seen unexpectedly from behind. His position on a horse, however, makes sense, because Christ is placed high up on the cross, as on Imogen Stuart's later crucifix in Armagh Cathedral (No. 50).

48. Glenstal Abbey, County Limerick
1965
Twelfth Station of the Cross
Terracotta plaque by Benedict Tutty, OSB

Crucifixion scenes in Ireland are found in great numbers on the Twelfth Station of the Cross. Many of the nineteenth-century plaster examples were executed in an undistinguished realism intended to extract the maximum effect on the sentimental emotions—but they generally are works of piety rather than of art. The twentieth century, in contrast, has seen a new artistic approach that is more stylized and infinitely more pleasing to the senses. One example, by Séamus Murphy (No. 43), we have already seen. Another very evocative and personal response is the Twelfth Station by the late Benedict Tutty, a monk of the Benedictine abbey of Glenstal in County Limerick. His normal material was bronze, with which he made many sensitive crucifixes in the 1960s. For his crucifixion Station, however, he chose a more unusual medium, terracotta or baked clay, which is given a slightly uneven, almost gritty surface entirely in keeping with the subject. The whole composition presents a fascinating interplay of lines, recalling twelfth-century examples (Nos. 6–8), and the artist himself felt a strong Celtic influence, particularly in the figure of Christ. The understated cross and flanking figures provide a horizontal and vertical structure that is offset by diagonals seen not only in the loincloth but also in the Savior's body, his raised arms, and the lance piercing the wounds; the diagonals converge on the focal feature of Christ's head. Like a low cloud around a mountain top, the Crown of Thorns, feelingly indicated by deep gashes, hangs heavily above the Savior's furrowed brow, with the eyes closed in death beneath. Appropriately close to Christ's face is that of the Virgin, delicately showing the grief of the bereaved mother who is prevented from falling in a faint only by the supporting hand of St. John behind her. The somewhat unusual grouping of these two figures on the right places Christ slightly off-center, and leaves the left-hand side free for the invisibly held lance. The Gothic crossed feet reinforce the dignified sorrow of the scene that this panel so vividly expresses.

48. Dick Deegan

49. By courtesy of Ken Thompson

49. Ken Thompson
1980
Rubbing

In contrast to the thousands of lurid and sentimental template-made crucifixion-tombstones that clutter our cemeteries today, there are very few crucifixions that have been chiseled by Irish stone carvers of originality in our own century. As we have seen, even the doyen Séamus Murphy is known to have produced only one (No. 43). All the more is it to be welcomed that a member of the younger generation, upon whom the mantle of Séamus Murphy has fallen, now continues the age-old tradition of carving artistically in stone. This is Ken Thompson, a sculptor born in Cork in 1946, and who is the youngest of all the artists whose crucifixes are illustrated in this volume. For the sake of variety, though, it is a rubbing rather than a stone carving of his that is chosen for reproduction here. His work is full of natural and unaffected charm, and he is one of the few carvers remaining in Ireland who delights in producing hand-carved lettering that is both easy to read and aesthetically a joy to behold. This can be sensed in the letters NIKA beneath Christ's feet on the rubbing opposite. The word means victory in Greek and it proclaims Christ's defeat of death and the devil. The hands placed above the cross and loosed from their nails in a gesture of acclaim announce the presence here of the Triumphant Christ, his hair-draped face evoking a confident compassion for those whom he has come to save. The solid and mildly undulating contours of the Savior's body are gracefully off-set by the diagonal folds of the loincloth, the left-hand side of which bears what is perhaps no more than a fortuitous resemblance to a harp. Thompson carved a stone variant of this composition for the Edmund Ignatius Rice Chapel at Mount Sion in Waterford.

50. St. Patrick's Roman Catholic Cathedral, Armagh
1984
Large bronze crucifix by Imogen Stuart (born 1927)

Imogen Stuart is a sculptress of German origin who has made Ireland her home for forty years. By 1957 she had made a profound impression with her Romanesque-inspired bronze panels for the west doorway of Galway Cathedral. Since then, she has established a reputation as one of the foremost of the all-too-few serious artists actively involved in the creation of religious art in Ireland, producing a number of remarkable works that have provided attractive furnishings for the spate of modern churches built in the country since the 1950s. Her most recent work includes one of the largest crucifixes ever to have been made in Ireland. Commissioned by Cardinal Ó Fiaich, through the architect Liam MacCormick, it now hangs on one of the pillars of the Catholic Cathedral in Armagh. Made of bronze, the cross is in the shape of a tree, with a single branch forking upward on either side, alluding to the anti-nuclear logo. The simple yet moving figure of the crucified Christ hangs high up on the cross. He is clothed only in a mildly folded loincloth, and his long, thin arms call forth our compassion, yet the dignified, stylized, and haloed head of the Savior expresses a nobility that portrays a Christ more of triumph than of pity. This turning away from the suffering Christ, which has dominated crucifixes since the Gothic period in the thirteenth century, is gently emphasized—as in the Harry Clarke window in Terenure (No. 44)—by the placing of Christ's feet side by side in the earlier Romanesque fashion, when the emphasis was also on Christ's victory. Of her crucifix, the artist herself says: "My Christ for Armagh Cathedral is cruciform. Christ is the cross—symbol of salvation—savior of men—embracing all humanity. He is the resurrection after suffering, nailed to the tree of life—stem of Jesse—tree of mankind. His elongated body gives the figure an upsurging movement, and the shrouded face tells of God's mystery and his revelation in Christ."

96

50. Michael Campbell, Armagh, by courtesy of Imogen Stuart and the Catholic Archbishop of Armagh

Additional Notes to the Text and Illustrations

Nos. 1 and 3: For a discussion, including the dating, of these two pieces, see P. Harbison, "The bronze Crucifixion plaque said to be from St. John's (Rinnagan), near Athlone," *The Journal of Irish Archeology* II (1984): 1–17.

Nos. 2, 4, 9, and 10: For further details on these four crosses, see P. Harbison, *The High Crosses of Ireland* (Bonn: Habelt, 1992).

No. 5: For the latest discussion, see P. Harbison, "The Date of the Crucifixion slabs from Duvillaun More and Inishkea North, Co. Mayo," in (Ed. E. Rynne), *Figures from the Past, Studies in Figurative Art in Christian Ireland in honor of Helen M. Roe* (Dún Laoghaire: Glendale Press, 1987), 73ff.

Nos. 6 and 7: See P. Harbison, "A lost Crucifixion plaque of Clonmacnoise type found in Co. Mayo," in (Ed. H. Murtagh), *Irish Midland Studies, Essays in Commemoration of N. W. English* (Athlone: The Old Athlone Society, 1980), 24–38 and Cormac Bourke, "The chronology of Irish Crucifixion plaques," in (Ed. R.M. Spearman and J. Higgitt), *The Age of Migrating Ideas* (Edinburgh and Stroud: National Museums of Scotland and Alan Sutton Publishing, 1993), 175–81. The provenance of the Marrassit or College plaque from County Tyrone has been demonstrated in Ann Hamlin and R. G. Haworth, "A Crucifixion Plaque Re-provenanced," *Journal of the Royal Society of Antiquaries of Ireland* 112 (1982): 112–115.

No. 8: For the latest discussion, see Susanne McNab, "The Romanesque Figure Sculpture at Maghera, County Derry and Raphoe, County Donegal," in (Ed. J. Fenlon, N. Figgis and C. Marshall), *New Perspectives, Studies in Art History in honor of Anne Crookshank* (Dublin: Irish Academic Press, 1987), 19–33, and P. Harbison, "The biblical iconography of Irish Romanesque architectural sculpture," in (Ed. C. Bourke), *From the Isles of the North, Early Medieval Art in Ireland and Britain* (Belfast: Her Majesty's Stationery Office, 1995), 271–281. For the continental crucifixions with numerous figures, see Gertrud Schiller, *Iconography of Christian Art, Volume 2, The Passion of Jesus Christ,* (London: Lund Humphries, 1972), which has provided many useful thoughts for the present work.

No. 11: See R. Ó Floinn, "Irish Romanesque Crucifix Figures," in (Ed. E. Rynne), *Figures from the Past, Studies in Figurative Art in Christian Ireland in Honor of Helen M. Roe* (Dún Laoghaire: Glendale Press, 1987), 168–88.

No. 12: See G. L. Barrow, *The Round Towers of Ireland* (Dublin: Academy Press, 1979), 162–66.

No. 13: J. Hunt, *Irish Medieval Figure Sculpture* (London/Dublin: Sotheby/Irish University Press, 1974), Vol. 1, 206, No. 188.

No. 15: I am grateful to Miss M. Ní Dhomhnalláin for bringing this drawing to my notice.

No. 16: G. Carville, *The Heritage of Holy Cross* (Belfast: Blackstaff Press, 1973), 44 and 51.

No. 17: H. M. Roe, *Medieval Fonts of Meath* (Meath Archaeological and Historical Society, 1968), 19–20 and 36–45.

No. 18: Hunt, op. cit., 122.

No. 19: R. Ó. Floinn, "Gilt Silver Processional Cross," in (Ed. M. Ryan) *Treasures of Ireland, Irish Art 3000 BC–1500 AD* (Dublin: Royal Irish Academy, 1983), 181–82.

No. 20: H. King, "Late medieval crosses in County Meath, *c.* 1470–1635," *Proceedings of the Royal Irish Academy* 84 C. 1984: 105.

No. 21: After E. Ledwich, *The Antiquities of Ireland,* 2nd ed. (London: 1804), opp. p. 520.

No. 22: M. Wynne, "The Irish Archaeological Inspiration of Evie Hone," *Journal of the County Kildare Archaeological Society* 14, No. 2, 1966–67: 246–47 and H. King, "The medieval and seventeenth century carved stone collection in Kildare," *Journal of the Co. Kildare Archaeological Society* 17 (1987-91): 83–85, No. 16.

No. 23: P. Ó hÉailidhe, "Fassaroe and Associated Crosses," *Journal of the Royal Society of Antiquaries of Ireland* 88 (1958): 101–10.

No. 24: Hunt, op. cit., 161–63, No. 89c.

No. 25: Hunt, op. cit., 189, No. 145c.

No. 26: Hunt, op. cit., 180, No. 126.

No. 27: Hunt, op. cit., 210–11, No. 196.

No. 28: H. King, "The medieval and seventeenth-century carved stone collection in Kildare," *Journal of the County Kildare Archaeological Society* 17 (1987–91): 87–89, No. 23.

No. 29: P. McSwiney, "The Defeat of the Church in Penal Kinsale," *Journal of the Cork Historical and Archaeological Society* 46 (1941): 102–03; *Guide to St. Multose Church, Kinsale*, 2nd ed., 1961.

No. 32: H. King, "Irish wayside and churchyard crosses 1600–1700," *Post-Medieval Archaeology* 19 (1985): 13–33. For continental parallels for the Christ with raised arms, see Erich Hubala, *Die Kunst des 17 Jahrhunderts,* Propyläen Kunstgeschichte 9 (Berlin: Propyläen Verlag, 1970), 299–300, No. 346, with Ab. 346 and A. O'Rahilly, *The Crucified* (Dublin: Kingdom Books, 1985), Illustration X, 21.

No. 33: J. O'Connor, *St. Mary's Abbey, Ballyhaunis* (Ballyhaunis: Augustinian Community, 1983), 5.

No. 34: Heather A. King, "Seventeenth Century Effigial Sculpture in the North Meath Area," in (Ed. E. Rynne), *Figures from the Past, Studies on Figurative Art in Christian Ireland in honor of Helen M. Roe* (Dún Laoghaire: Glendale Press, 1987), 302–03.

No. 35: W. FitzGerald, "The Browne Mausoleum at Mainham," *Journal of the County Kildare Archaeological Society* III, No. 4 (1901): 260–64; Maurice Craig and Michael Craig, *Mausolea Hibernica* (Dublin: Lilliput Press, 1999), 21–2.

No. 36: Compare the Mooney tombstone by Dennis Cullen in the same graveyard—Maurice Craig and the Knight of Glin, *Ireland Observed* (Cork: Mercier Press, 1970), 97. For the story of the cock and the pot, see A. T. Lucas, *Penal Crucifixes* (Dublin: Stationery Office, 1958), 27–28.

No. 37: A. Crookshank, *Irish Sculpture from 1600 to the present day* (Dublin: Department of Foreign Affairs, 1984), 30.

No. 38: Compare Lucas, op. cit.

Nos. 39 and 40: A. K. Longfield (Mrs. H.G. Leask), *Some Irish Churchyard Sculpture* (Ballycotton: Gifford and Craven, 1974), 23–28.

No. 43: *Séamus Murphy 1907–75* (no date), 65, No. 355.

No. 44: (Ed. J. Healy), *Stained-Glass Memorial Window, St. Joseph's, Terenure, Souvenir of Dedication* (Dublin, 1920). Fr. Healy lists the Irish saints as follows: Left-hand side: SS Coga, Braccan, Erc, Conlaeth, Kevin, Ita, Sedulius, Fintan, Berac, Patrick, and Colga; right-hand side: SS Munchin, Albert, Gobinet, Attracta, Laurence, Brendan, Fechin, Colman, Finnbar, and Brigid. Nicola Gordon Bowe, in *Harry Clarke* (Exhibition Catalogue) (Dublin, 1979), 31, notes that Clarke used photographs taken of himself as the model for the figure of Christ. See also Nicola Gordon Bowe, David Caron, and Michael Wynne, *Gazetteer of Irish Stained Glass* (Blackrock: Irish Academic Press, 1988), 53. I am grateful to Eithne Waldron for bringing this window to my attention.

No. 45: The quotations are from Mainie Jellett, "I sought the inner principle," in (Ed. S. Frost) *A Tribute to Evie Hone and Mainie Jellett* (Dublin: Browne and Nolan, 1957), 66. See also (Ed. E. MacCarvill), *Mainie Jellett: The Artist's Vision* (Dundalk: Dundalgan Press, 1958), Pl. III, and *Mainie Jellett (1897–1944), A Retrospective Exhibition of Paintings and Drawings,* Municipal Gallery of Modern Art (Dublin: July–October 1962), 26, No. 66. I am grateful to Pádraig Ó Táillúir for bringing this painting to my attention.

No. 46: See the book edited by Stella Frost quoted in the previous note, and Gordon Bowe, Caron, and Wynne, op. cit., 36. The older Irish stone carvings (including some crucifixion scenes illustrated in this volume) that Evie Hone sketched are listed in M. Wynne, "The Irish Archaeological Inspiration of Evie Hone," *Journal of the County Kildare Archaeological Society* 14 (1966–67), 247–53.

No. 48: Compare M. Wynne, "Forward," *Sacred Art 1* (1961), 2–3.

No. 49: Ken Thompson's stone crucifix in Waterford, with its echoes of the work of Benedict Tutty, is illustrated in (Ed. R. Knowles) *Contemporary Irish Art* (Dublin: Wolfhound Press; New York: St. Martin's Press, 1982), No. 115.

About the author

Professor Peter Harbison worked with the Irish Tourist Board as an archaeologist and, later, as editor of its international magazine, *Ireland of the Welcomes*. He is professor of archaeology at the Royal Hibernian Academy of Art and honorary academic editor of the Royal Irish Academy. His many books on Irish art and archaeology include *The High Crosses of Ireland* (1992), *Ancient Ireland* (co-author, 1996) and *The Golden Age of Irish Art* (1999).

The text of this book is set in Mrs. Eaves, a digital version of
a typeface designed by John Baskerville around 1758.

The headlines and display matter are set in Centaur,
a typeface designed by Bruce Rogers in 1915,
based on Nicholas Jenson's 15th century type.